D0579178

The Ultimate Round

18 Life Lessons from the World's Greatest Golfers

Text by Terry Glaspey
Paintings by Larry Dyke

HARVEST HOUSE PUBLISHERS

EUGENE, OREGON

The Ultimate Round
Text copyright © 2004 by Terry Glaspey
Published by Harvest House Publishers
Eugene, Oregon 97402
www.harvesthousepublishers.com

Library of Congress Cataloging-in-Publication Data

Glaspey, Terry W.
  The ultimate round / text by Terry Glaspey; paintings by Larry Dyke.
     p. cm.
ISBN 0-7369-1276-2
1. Golf—Moral and ethical aspects. 2. Golfers—Conduct of life.
3. Golfers—Portraits. I. Title.
GV965.G39 2004
796.352—dc22
                    2003015526

Terry Glaspey has also authored *Where the Grass Is Always Greener: Insight and Inspiration from the Fairway*
(also available from Harvest House Publishers), as well as seven other books.

Artwork copyright © by Larry Dyke and may not be reproduced without the artist's permission.

Design and production by Koechel Peterson & Associates, Inc., Minneapolis, Minnesota

Harvest House Publishers and the author have made every effort to trace the ownership of all quotes. In the event of a question arising from the use of a quote, we regret any error made and will be pleased to make the necessary correction in future editions of this book.

All rights reserved. No part of this publication may be reproduced, stored in a retrieval system, or transmitted in any form or by any means—electronic, mechanical, digital, photocopy, recording, or any other—except for brief quotations in printed reviews, without the prior permission of the publisher.

Contents

18 HOLES FOR THE SOUL

elcome to a golf course you'll never actually get to play. That is, unless you have the unlimited time and money to fly all over the country to play each course that is represented here! For the rest of us, reading this book will have to do. Actually, the course you are about to play exists only in the realm of the imagination. But if you choose, you can also experience it in the realm of the soul.

We've taken the beautiful paintings of Larry Dyke to represent 18 holes of an ideal course and paired them with thoughts about the personal growth we can experience when we learn some of the lessons golf can teach us.

Following a custom seen at many of the greatest courses, each of these holes has been given its own name—one that's unique to our imaginary course, not related to the name the hole might have at its home course. These names represent 18 character qualities that will not only make us more successful golfers, but also—if we practice them—make us more successful in the game of life. Some of the qualities that will shave a few strokes off your score are also invaluable in becoming the kind of person we all most likely want to be: happy, successful, and spiritually mature.

Since this is an ideal course, why not make our imaginary round even better by imagining the ideal companions for our round: some of the greatest golfers who ever lived? At each hole we will be joined by a famous golfer who exemplifies in some way the quality represented by that hole. For example, on the hole named "Focus," we'll be accompanied by Ben Hogan—a man whose ability to focus was one of the keys to his extraordinary success. Because we usually learn best from mentors, those who have excelled and can pass on their wisdom and example, who better to mentor us in improving our game—and our life—than men and women like Hogan, Palmer, Sorenstam, Nicklaus, and Woods?

Along the way, we'll also take a look at the records of these champions and get some further advice from the gallery (quotes from other greats and assorted golf nuts—all records for tournament victories are as of June 1, 2003). If you think of reading this book as though you are playing the ultimate round, with the stakes being improved character and a better life, then you'll realize that the 18 holes ahead of us are no simple layout that can be mastered by one trip through. No—this lifetime journey will, with each successive round, see us refining our skills and getting better and better. And though it's a tough course, I'm sure you're up for the challenge!

"If just some of the sensible principles that keep golfers out of trouble in their day-to-day affairs were applied to their games, their handicaps would drop drastically."

—Greg Norman

"By and large, your golf game mirrors your personality."

—Lanny Wadkins

FINDING PLEASURE

— Arnold Palmer —

More than anyone else in the history of golf, Arnold Palmer was responsible for bringing the game to the masses. His appeal was down-to-earth, even blue-collar, and he showed you didn't have to be part of the cultural elite to fall in love with the game. Palmer brought a new kind of excitement to golf. He single-handedly made the sport more popular with his swashbuckling, go-for-broke style and by demonstrating a passion that was contagious. "I'm in love with golf," he once said, "and I want everybody else to share my love affair."

And share it we did, watching him slash at the ball with his mighty swing and his uniquely off-kilter follow-through, or sharing his infectious enthusiasm as he holed a critical putt. His fans were so legion that the press nicknamed them "Arnie's Army." And they always enjoyed cheering him on, especially when he made one of his come-from-behind charges—like when he shot 65 to win the U.S. Open in 1960 after starting the last round seven strokes back.

Palmer always looked like he was having fun, finding enjoyment in every stroke he played. He found challenge in the complexity of the game, delight in the beauties of the courses, and excitement in the way it aroused his competitive nature. For Palmer, golfing *was* pleasure!

In life as in golf, we should take the time to enjoy the circumstances we are in, be challenged rather than overcome by life's difficulties, and seek the pleasure that comes from sharing the joys we discover with others.

> "What a beautiful place a golf course is. From the meanest country pasture to the Pebble Beaches and St. Andrews of the world, a golf course is to me a holy ground. I feel God in the trees and grass and flowers, in the rabbits and the birds and the squirrels, in the sky and the water. I feel that I am home."
>
> —HARVEY PENICK

> "I don't play golf to feel bad.
> I play bad golf and still feel good."
>
> —LESLIE NIELSEN

> "I have a tip that can take five strokes off
> anyone's golf game. It's called an eraser."
>
> —ARNOLD PALMER

The Palmer Scorecard

Major Championship Victories

U.S. Amateur (1955)
Masters (1958, 1960, 1962, 1964)
U.S. Open (1960)
British Open (1961, 1962)

Other Significant Achievements

Winner of 60 PGA Tour events
PGA Player of the Year (1960, 1962)
Vardon Trophy Winner (1961, 1962, 1964, 1967)

CONFIDENCE

— Walter Hagen —

Walter Hagen was golf's greatest showman and a player of supreme confidence. A natty dresser, when he donned his white flannel golf slacks, he brought a sense of style to the stuffy world of professional golf. "Sir Walter," as he was sometimes dubbed, was also the first full-time tournament professional.

He was a man of grand and memorable gestures. In his day, the playing professionals were not honored very highly by the clubs hosting the tournament events. In fact, professionals were generally not respected enough to be allowed in the clubhouse. When Hagen won the 1922 British Open at Royal St. George's, he was turned away when he tried to use the members' locker room. Undaunted, he hired an Austro-Daimler limousine and parked it right in front of the clubhouse. He climbed into the backseat to change his clothes and had a fine gourmet meal delivered to the vehicle.

Hagen's greatest asset was his unshakeable confidence that he could win any time he teed up the ball. As the great golf writer Herbert Warren Wind noted, "Walter Hagen had a sterling contempt for second place. He believed that the public only remembered a winner, that a man might as well be tenth as second when the shooting was over."

For a time, Hagen seemed all but unbeatable, especially at match play. When the PGA Championship was still a match-play event, he won it an unparalleled four times in a row! En route to these victories, he won 22 straight 36-hole matches. Perhaps the secret to his winning ways in the match-play format was his mastery of the psych-out. For example, when he was in a bunker off the green, he would usually ask his caddie to remove the flagstick before he played the shot. He wanted his opponent to know he believed he could hole the shot.

In life as in golf, we must have confidence in ourselves if we want to achieve great things or find success. Confidence leads to decisiveness, an important trait for making the most of our lives. We shouldn't allow ourselves to be paralyzed by the what-ifs of life. Sometimes we just need to make a decision and have the confidence to live with the results.

"It is more important to be decisive than to be correct when preparing to play any golf shot."

—BOB ROTELLA

"Fear ruins more golf shots, for duffer and star, than any other factor."

—TOMMY ARMOUR

HOLE #2

*"Confidence is everything. From there,
it's a small step to winning."*

—CRAIG STADLER

*"Be decisive. A wrong decision is generally
less disastrous than indecision."*

—BERNHARD LANGER

*"Sometimes we get so afraid of hitting bad shots
we don't let ourselves hit good ones."*

—BUTCH HARMON

The Hagen Scorecard

Major Championship Victories

U.S. Open (1914, 1919)
PGA Championship (1921, 1924, 1925, 1926, 1927)
British Open (1922, 1924, 1928, 1929)

Other Significant Achievements

Winner of 40 PGA Tour events, including 5
victories in the Western Open at a time when
it was widely considered a major.

A BIGGER VISION

— Tiger Woods —

By the time he took the golf world by storm, those who had been paying attention had already seen him coming. Tiger Woods had been taught the game at a very early age, and his uncanny abilities manifested themselves almost immediately. His father had groomed him to be a golf prodigy, and he was—he has turned out to be one of the very finest players the game has ever seen.

After dominating the world of junior golf (three straight U.S. Junior Championships in 1991, 1992, and 1993), Tiger went on to win the same number of U.S. Amateur Championships in a row. Having established himself as the best at every amateur level, he was soon recognized as the best professional golfer of the twenty-first century, winning each of the professional Grand Slam tournaments at least once. In fact, in what has been dubbed the "Tiger Slam," at one point, Woods held the title of champion in all four major events at the same time. His streak of play from 1999 through 2001 was nothing less than spectacular. Some are already prepared to give him the title of "the greatest player in the history of the game."

All this success did not come about by chance. It was the result of Tiger's bigger vision for the kind of golfer he wanted to be. He didn't want to be just a good golfer. He wanted to be the best. So he set countless goals for himself, initially focusing on breaking as many of Jack Nicklaus's career records as possible. As a young man, he posted those records in his room, using them to spur himself on to outdo the man who has long been considered the greatest golfer ever. Many of those goals have now been checked off. And who is to say that Tiger might not eclipse Nicklaus's once seemingly unbeatable record of major championship victories…

Tiger holds his goal of being the very best golfer he can be as a single-minded passion. His pursuit of improvement in every element of his game is relentless. After his record-breaking win in the 1997 Masters, when many golfers might have chosen to rest on their laurels, Woods decided his basic swing was not good enough—so he completely rebuilt it. This created a short dry spell in winnings, but once he finally mastered the new swing, his game was better than ever!

In life as in golf, we need to have a bigger vision and keep our goals in front of us if we want to achieve our full potential. What goals do you have? Do these goals involve your character and your soul? If you have a healthy vision for the kind of person you want to become, a purposeful focus makes it much more likely that you'll accomplish your goals.

"I see no reason why a golf course cannot be played in 18 birdies. Just because no one has ever done that doesn't mean it can't be done."

—BEN HOGAN

"Golf is not a game of great shots. It's a game of the most accurate misses. The people who win make the smallest mistakes."

—GENE LITTLER

"Golf is 20 percent talent and 80 percent management."

—BEN HOGAN

The Woods Scorecard

Major Championship Victories

U.S. Amateur (1994, 1995, 1996)
Masters (1997, 2001, 2002)
PGA Championship (1999, 2000)
U.S. Open (2000, 2002)
British Open (2000)

Other Significant Achievements

Winner of 37 PGA Tour events
Vardon Trophy Winner (1999, 2000, 2001)
Player of the Year (1997, 1999, 2000, 2001, 2002)

DISCIPLINE

— Gary Player —

Some of the greatest golfers seem as if they are naturals—as though they were born with just the right set of golfing talents. But for most of us, becoming a better golfer is a matter of hard work, practice, and discipline. No golfer is a better example of the benefit of a focused work ethic than Gary Player. "I had a great deal of talent," he noted, "but talent alone will only take you so far."

Long before it was standard for PGA golfers to give much thought to physical conditioning, Player undertook a strict routine of practice, exercise, and healthy eating. He once laughingly credited his many victories to peanuts, bananas, and weight lifting. Keeping his health in order led to his retaining his competitive edge over the years. He is the only player in the history of the game to have won the British Open in three different decades. And in 1965 Player became only the third player in history to complete a career Grand Slam. As he once said, "The harder you work, the luckier you get."

Player's successful career is a living demonstration of the importance of consistent, focused practice. You get better only as you train yourself through repetition and adjustment. There is no hope of improving your game unless you spend a large amount of time practicing. Like Player, all good golfers are truly at home on the range.

In life as in golf, we'll improve our skills and our character only when we pay attention to our weaknesses and work to strengthen them. The lazy person will be like the lazy golfer—always stuck in the rut of the same bad habits. These bad habits are overcome only as they are replaced with good ones. And good habits come by practicing them consistently.

"I have proved to myself what I have always said—that a good golfer doesn't have to be born that way. He can be made. I was, and practice is what made me—practice and tough, unrelenting labor."

—BEN HOGAN

*"There is nothing in this game of golf that
can't be improved upon—if you practice."*

—PATTY BERG

*"Practice well, until you
don't have to think."*

—CALVIN PEETE

*"Confidence comes from working
extremely hard."*

—LEE TREVINO

*"Practice puts brains
in your muscles."*

—SAM SNEAD

The Player Scorecard

Major Championship Victories

U.S. Open (1965)
Masters (1961, 1974, 1978)
British Open (1959, 1968, 1972)
PGA Championship (1962, 1972)

Other Significant Achievements

Winner of 21 PGA Tour events
Winner of 163 tournaments worldwide

INTENSITY

— Jack Nicklaus —

There was something in those steely eyes of his. When you looked into them you saw a fierce intelligence and something more: a focused intensity. Jack Nicklaus—perhaps the greatest golfer of all time—had many gifts: power combined with finesse, a supreme gift for course management, and grace under pressure. But his most defining characteristic was his intensity. Jack took the game seriously and marshaled all his resources toward winning.

It is impossible to play your best golf all the time—golf is much too fickle a sport for that—but Nicklaus managed so often to find a way to win. As he once said to Tiger Woods, "I seldom won with my 'A' game. I won with my 'B' game and my 'C' game, and I managed." Manage he did. Beginning with his play-off victory over Arnold Palmer in the 1962 U.S. Open (at the young age of 22), he went on to win a total of 18 majors from 1962 through 1986.

Whether he was shooting a final-round 64 to win or struggling home with a 77, Nicklaus always retained his intensity. He took each shot seriously and never gave up. He never lost his focus. I recently saw some black-and-white footage of one of his victories in the U.S. Open. As Nicklaus stood over an important putt, the wind was howling, scattering leaves across the green. You could see his trousers flapping like a flag in the stiff breeze. Yet he stood perfectly still over that putt, with such intense concentration that when a gust blew his hat completely off his head he didn't even flinch. Of course, he made that putt…

In life as in golf, achievement is usually related to the intensity of our desire. To accomplish anything we must be serious about it and not allow ourselves to be distracted. What goals do you have that deserve—and need—this kind of intensity?

"One thing you don't ever want to do is think of bad things when you're over a ball. People might think about bad shots, but I don't—even on shots I might be scared to hit."

—FRED COUPLES

HOLE #5

"Many shots are spoiled at the last instant
by efforts to add a few more yards."

—BOBBY JONES

"One of the worst mistakes you can
make in golf is trying to force the game."

—JACK NICKLAUS

"Nicklaus was able to put himself in an intense frame
of mind, where nothing breaks his concentration and
he can almost will the ball into the hole."

—BEN CRENSHAW

The Nicklaus Scorecard

Major Championship Victories

U.S. Amateur (1959, 1961)
U.S. Open (1962, 1967, 1972, 1980)
Masters (1963, 1965, 1966, 1972, 1975, 1986)
British Open (1966, 1970, 1978)
PGA Championship (1963, 1971, 1973, 1975, 1980)

Other Significant Achievements

Winner of 70 PGA Tour events
PGA Player of the Year (1964, 1965, 1967, 1971,
1972, 1973, 1975, 1976)

BALANCE

— Sam Snead —

Fluidity, grace, beauty—these words describe the golf swing of "Slammin' Sammy" Snead, owner of what may be the best swing in the history of golf. That beautiful swing probably explains his incredible longevity in the winner's circle. At the ripe age of 62, he still had the talent to contend (and take third place) in the 1974 PGA Championship—28 years after his first major victory.

When asked about the secret to his swing, he once replied, "I try to feel oily." This smoothness led baseball great Ted Williams to remark, "Everyone who ever saw him swing a golf club knew they'd seen something to remember."

Everyone who has ever struggled to improve their golf swing knows that one of the key elements is balance. If you want to see balance in action, just watch the old films of Sam Snead. Without balance, you'll hack away at the ball and never find the tempo and poise that marked his elegant swing.

Snead also brought a sense of balance to his attitude toward the game. He knew golf wasn't everything. In fact, the main reason he played competitive golf, he said, was so he could afford to hunt and fish. And yet, by keeping his priorities in focus, Snead was able to win more tournaments than anyone else in the history of professional golf.

In life as in golf, we need to strive for a sense of balance, the poise that comes from keeping everything in proper perspective, that helps it all work together. Without balance, life can become one-dimensional—lacking richness, depth, and variety. Are there areas you need to bring into balance so you can live a better life?

"Grip pressure is very important. You can't strangle the club with a hog killer's grip. You've got to hold it as if it were a little bird—gently but firmly. You don't want it to fly away, but you don't want to suffocate the poor thing, either."

—SAM SNEAD

"When I swing at a golf ball right, my mind is blank and my body is loose as a goose."

—SAM SNEAD

"A good swing is a physical pleasure."

—BEN HOGAN

"Sam's always been smart enough to know that the surest way to ruin his swing would be to start getting too complex about it. He's kept his thinking simple."

—CARY MIDDLECOFF

The Snead Scorecard

Major Championship Victories
Masters (1949, 1952, 1954)
British Open (1946)
PGA Championship (1942, 1949, 1951)

Other Significant Achievements
Winner of 81 PGA Tour events
Vardon Trophy Winner (1938, 1949, 1950, 1955)

PATIENCE

— Tom Watson —

Ben Hogan said that he hit only five or six shots per round exactly as he intended. Isn't that an apt commentary on the game of golf? Once in a while, that little white ball does just exactly what we want it to. More often, we are the victims of slight mis-hits, terrible bounces, and plain old bad luck. That's why, as someone once said, golf is a game of managing your misses and avoiding disasters. In other words, the sport requires an incredible amount of patience.

Tom Watson had his share of bad breaks and periods during which he didn't seem able to play at his normal level, but he rarely lost his composure. Watson's patience, commented Tony Jacklin, made "all the difference." It was one of the secrets to his amazing success.

Chi Chi Rodriguez has observed that "golf is a game of endless predicaments." You never know what it's going to throw at you. Allowing yourself to get angry and frustrated does nothing to help your game. In fact, it makes your muscles tighten up and causes you to lose your focus, generally creating more mis-hits and mental errors. One characteristic common to the very greatest golfers is their placidity on the course—they take their time, they don't allow themselves to get rattled, they play one shot at a time.

Watson's patience served him well throughout his career. Who can ever forget his epic duel with Jack Nicklaus in the last two rounds of the 1977 British Open? He shot 65-65 to beat Nicklaus, who shot 65-66. Third place for that tournament (Hubert Green) was a distant eleven strokes back.

In life as in golf, we will experience more success, build better relationships, and find more joy if we cultivate the quality of patience. Patience comes from learning not to expect perfection out of everyone and out of every situation, but from being willing to accept the fact that bad things sometimes happen…and that real change can take time.

"Good golfing temperament falls between taking it with a grin or shrug and throwing a fit."

—SAM SNEAD

HOLE #7

"It is nothing new or original to say that golf is played one stroke at a time. But it took me many years to realize it."

—Bobby Jones

"The least thing upset him on the links. He missed short putts because of the uproar of butterflies in the adjoining meadows."

—P.G. Wodehouse

The Watson Scorecard

Major Championship Victories

Masters (1977, 1981)
U.S. Open (1982)
British Open (1975, 1977, 1980, 1982, 1983)

Other Significant Achievements

Winner of 34 PGA Tour events
Vardon Trophy Winner (1977, 1978, 1979)

DESIRE FOR IMPROVEMENT

— Mickey Wright —

*T*here can be little argument that Mickey Wright was the greatest female golfer of all time. No male golfer stood head and shoulders above his competitors as Wright did above hers. She retired only ten years after her first victory—with a total of 82 victories, including 13 women's majors. In the year 1963 alone she won an amazing 13 tournaments!

Her secret was her constant striving for improvement. She never settled for the level of playing she had already achieved. She always wanted to be better, was always driven to be the very best she could be.

Above all else, Wright strove to attain perfection in her golf swing. She practiced incessantly, working to develop the ideal ball flight (maximum carry with a slight draw that would land softly on the green). She knew that the golf swing was not just about power, but about technique—and technique was something that could always be improved. As she said, "You can't take a car from a dead stop and put it immediately up to 70 miles per hour. No matter how powerful your engine, you must have a gradual acceleration of speed. So it is in a golf swing."

Wright showed us that constant improvement is what makes this game so challenging and fun. If we ever settle for "good enough," we'll never reach our full potential.

In life as in golf, there is always room for change, improvement, and growth. We should develop the attitude that says, *I never need to accept the status quo or use it as an excuse. I can be better—a better person, a better mate, a better parent.* Do you want your life to be just "good enough," or do you want it to be a masterpiece?

> *"I feel as if I've earned my own version of a master's degree in psychology, in study and experience, trial and error, on golf courses throughout the United States. For psychology…is as integral a part of good golf as an efficient swing."*
>
> —MICKEY WRIGHT

"It is the constant and undying hope for improvement
that makes golf so exquisitely worth playing."

—BERNARD DARWIN

"Putting is like wisdom—partly a natural gift
and partly the accumulation of experience."

—ARNOLD PALMER

"Don't be too proud to take lessons. I'm not."

—JACK NICKLAUS

"All golfers, men and women, professional and amateur,
are united by one thing: their desire to improve."

—JUDY RANKIN

The Wright Scorecard

Major Championship Victories

U.S. Women's Open (1958, 1959, 1961, 1964)
LPGA Championship (1958, 1960, 1961, 1963)
Titleholders Championship (1961, 1962)
Western Open (1962, 1963, 1966)

Other Significant Achievements

Winner of 84 LPGA Tour events
Vare Trophy Winner (1960, 1961, 1962, 1963, 1964)
Associated Press Woman Athlete of the Year (1962, 1963)

FOCUS

— Ben Hogan —

Ben Hogan was a marvelous shot maker. Jack Nicklaus once said that when it came to any of the 14 clubs in the bag, no one showed more overall talent with them than Hogan. But what allowed him to marshal this talent so he could win tournaments was his focus. He knew that golf was played one shot at a time. His ability to single-mindedly focus on the next shot before him—and nothing else—was legendary. What you had just done or what was to come was never as important as the shot you were playing now. On being asked what was the most important shot in golf, he answered, "The next one."

Hogan's concentration was such that he barely spoke while he was on the course. Sam Snead said that usually the only words he spoke during a round when they played together were these: "You're away." Ben focused on his own game and didn't worry about what others were doing. In fact, Lloyd Mangrum relates that while playing in a tournament with Hogan, he watched him put his tee shot fairly close to the pin on a par three. Then Mangrum hit a perfect tee shot, which bounded right into the hole—a hole in one! They walked in silence to the green. Once they reached the putting surface, Mangrum plucked his ball from the hole and watched as Hogan narrowly missed his putt. As they walked off the green, he heard Hogan mutter something about his miss. It hadn't even registered with him that his playing partner had scored an ace!

In life as in golf, we need to learn to live in the present moment. If our focus lies on the past or is distracted by too much dreaming (or worrying) about the future, we may never find true happiness and meaning in our lives. Each moment is a precious gift given to us by God…it is such a shame to think we might miss the wonder of it because we are too busy replaying the past or planning for the future.

"I didn't play my best golf, but I kept focused better than I ever had. I stayed in the present tense all week."

—TOM KITE, AFTER WINNING THE 1992 U.S. OPEN

HOLE #9

"When I'm in this state, everything is pure, vividly clear. I'm in a cocoon of concentration."

—TONY JACKLIN

"You swing your best when you have the fewest things to think about."

—BOBBY JONES

"If you want to help yourself and the game, don't play slowly. Your concentration wanders."

—GENE SARAZEN

The Hogan Scorecard

Major Championship Victories

Masters (1951, 1953)
U.S. Open (1948, 1950, 1951, 1953)
British Open (1953)
PGA Championship (1946, 1948)

Other Significant Achievements

Winner of 68 PGA Tour events
PGA Player of the Year (1948, 1950, 1951, 1953)
Vardon Trophy Winner (1940, 1941, 1948)

HONOR

— Tom Kite —

During the 1993 Kemper Open, Tom Kite and Grant Waite were paired together in the third round. When Waite's ball landed in a ground-under-repair area, he was forced to take a drop. As he set up to take his next shot, he failed to notice that one of his feet was on the repair chalk line. Kite, who at the time led by a slim one-shot margin, saw this and warned Waite not to play the shot, pointing out that if he were to hit the ball from that stance he would incur a two-shot penalty for standing on the line. Waite thanked him, redropped, took a proper stance, and went on to win the tournament the next day—by one shot over Tom Kite.

When reporters credited Kite with his sportsmanship, he simply replied, "It would have been pretty chicken of me to see him break a rule and then say, 'By the way, Grant, add two strokes.' That's not golf. That's those other sports where they're trying to get away with everything."

Golf is an honorable game, and it is certainly the only professional sport where you'll see players call a penalty on themselves. Can you imagine an NFL cornerback calling a penalty on himself for pass interference? And yet, in golf it is not unusual to see this kind of honest act. Tom Kite always tried to be a gentleman when he played the game, for he knew that how you won was as important as winning itself.

In life as in golf, honor and honesty are crucially important, for they determine the kind of character we will develop in our lives. Honor means doing the right thing, even when no one may notice if we do the wrong thing. Honor understands that one of the greatest things in life is to be able to look in the mirror and see a person of integrity looking back at us.

"I used to play golf with a guy who cheated so badly that he once had a hole in one and wrote down zero on his scorecard."

—BOB BRUCE

"For most amateurs, the best wood in the bag is the pencil."

—CHI CHI RODRIGUEZ

HOLE #10

"Golf is like solitaire. When you cheat, you only cheat yourself."

—TONY LEMA

"Golf is a game in which you yell fore, shoot six, and write down five."

—PAUL HARVEY

"I'd like to be known as a gentleman first, and then as a golfer. That's all."

—BEN HOGAN

The Kite Scorecard

Major Championship Victories
U.S. Open (1992)

Other Significant Achievements
Winner of 19 PGA Tour events

GRACE UNDER PRESSURE

— Greg Norman —

ew golfers have had to deal with more disappointment and just plain old bad luck than Greg Norman. For all his achievements—and they are many—he is more often remembered for all his near-misses. He is the only golfer in history to have lost all four majors in play-offs. (And this is no disgrace—you have to remember it takes a lot of talent to put yourself in the position to win as often as he did.) But despite all the disappointments the game threw his way, Norman always remained dignified and composed in the face of his adversity.

In 1986 Norman was the leader going into the final round of all four majors. At the Masters, an errant tee shot on the approach to 18 allowed Jack Nicklaus to win. At the U.S. Open, he shot a miserable 78 for the final round and lost. At the PGA Championship, it looked like he had victory locked up—until Bob Tway holed an unlikely bunker shot on the final hole to win by one stroke. Finally, at the British Open that year, he found the victory he'd been pursuing all year long.

The next year at the Masters, it again looked like Norman might win, until Larry Mize chipped in from well off the green to again snatch victory from his grasp. And who can ever forget the 1996 Masters, where Norman led by six shots going into the final round, only to be overtaken by Nick Faldo as his game uncharacteristically collapsed? But what is just as memorable as this shattering defeat is the amazing poise, humility, and sportsmanship Norman demonstrated in dealing with the loss. His attitude showed both a clear perspective and honor for his opponent. In the weeks that followed he was showered by letters of consolation and encouragement. Many others found strength from his example of grace under pressure.

And it didn't cause Norman to give up, either. As he once said, "Sometimes I have an almost perverse love of being down, even being defeated, because I know it will spur me on to greater things."

In life as in golf, we must learn to accept the misfortune and disappointments that come our way. It is easy for us to focus on the failures and injustices of our past, but we will find much greater peace in our lives if we focus on the present and the future. Life is always going to throw difficulties our way, and the wise person is the one who learns to take them in stride.

"One of the most fascinating things about golf is how it reflects the cycle of life. No matter what you shoot, the next day you have to go back to the first tee and begin all over again and make yourself into something."

—PETER JACOBSEN

"Nothing is ever going to be perfect in this life. You have to expect a little detour now and then."

—GREG NORMAN

"Golf is the hardest game in the world. There's no way you can ever get it. Just when you think you do, the game jumps up and puts you in your place."

—PETER JACOBSEN

"You've got to gamble every once in a while in a round of golf. I'm not afraid to screw up."

—FUZZY ZOELLER

The Norman Scorecard

Major Championship Victories
British Open (1986, 1993)

Other Significant Achievements
Winner of 18 PGA Tour events
Winner of 57 tournaments worldwide
Vardon Trophy Winner (1988, 1989, 1994)
PGA Player of the Year (1995)

RELAXATION

— Fred Couples —

Ever wonder why the great golfers waggle the club before they make their shot? Many amateurs imitate this movement without really thinking about its purpose. The waggle not only helps you focus before the shot, it is also an aid to relaxation. It loosens the muscles—and tight muscles reduce flexibility and our sense of "touch," robbing us of what we need to make our best shot. We'll play our best when we're relaxed.

The ability to relax and take things in stride has helped make Fred Couples a golfer to be reckoned with. Couples nearly always seems to be unperturbed. He always looks like he is enjoying himself, winning over the fans with his honest and open smile. In the midst of a high-stakes, pressure-filled round of golf, his body language is more like that of a man out to enjoy the surroundings during a casual weekend round with his friends.

This relaxation manifests itself in his swing, which has an almost languid tempo. It looks effortless, with a little pause for power at the top of the backswing. And its results over the years have been impressive, making him a frequent winner on the PGA Tour. Plus, it's a lot of fun to watch someone play who seems to be enjoying himself so much!

No one who saw it will ever forget that shot to the twelfth green at Augusta during the 1992 Masters. As soon as Couples hit the shot, the gallery—which had been pulling for him all afternoon—was certain it was going to come up short. They'd already seen several other golfers' shots come up short and roll down the bank into the water that fronts the green on this famous hole. Well, Couple's shot did come up short, but—miraculously—it stayed put. Everyone held their breath as he got quickly to where his ball lay and lofted it onto the green. There was something magical about that moment, and it paved the way for him to win the tournament.

In life as in golf, worry, stress, and tension are seldom helpful emotions. If we can reach down inside ourselves and find some inner peace, we'll find the relaxed attitude that makes life a lot easier to bear…and a whole lot more fun.

"I do some form of breathing exercises during a pressure situation. It definitely helps. Every time, before I hit a key shot, I take a deep breath and cleanse the mind."

—PAUL AZINGER

HOLE #12

"I've tried to pay attention and not look around too much. But there's so much to look at."

—FRED COUPLES

"Don't hurry. Don't worry. You're only here on a short visit, so don't forget to stop and smell the flowers."

—WALTER HAGEN

"Just relax."

—ERNIE ELS

"A tense mind breeds tense muscles, and tense muscles make you feel clumsy, out of gear."

—JACK NICKLAUS

The Couples Scorecard

Major Championship Victories
Masters (1992)

Other Significant Achievements
Winner of 15 PGA Tour events

SELF-CONTROL

— Byron Nelson —

Speaking of Byron Nelson, Ken Venturi paid him this compliment: "Byron was the greatest gentleman the game has ever known. I never heard him swear, never saw him lose his temper, and was always amazed at the consideration he showed every person he met."

But Nelson was more than just a gentleman—he was one of the greatest golfers of all time. In 1945, this paragon of courtliness and grace won an astonishing 11 tournaments in a row, a record no one since has even come close to equaling. The very next year, after winning six tournaments, Nelson quietly retired, near the top of his game.

Many credit him with having the first modern-style golf swing. He hit the ball with amazing accuracy thanks to the almost machinelike repeatability of his swing. In one U.S. Open he hit the flagstick six times in 72 holes.

Nelson's remarkable accuracy is also connected with the sense of calm he displayed on the course. When you watch the best golfers play, you'll notice that one of the characteristics that most of them have in common is self-control. Golfers who explode, throw clubs, and curse their fate generally do not make it to the highest level in golf. When we get frustrated or embarrassed by a wayward shot, we tend to lose our composure—and with it, our ability to think straight and shoot straight.

In life as in golf, we must learn to control our emotions, or our emotions will control us. Outbursts of anger and frustration rarely do anything more than make a difficult situation that much harder to handle. When we can find an inner calm within our hearts, we'll be able to take better control of our lives and live by our choices rather than our reactions.

*"Golf cannot be played in anger, or in any mood of emotional excess.
Half the golf balls struck by amateurs are hit, if not in rage, surely in
bewilderment, or gloom, or cynicism, or even hysterically—all of those
emotional excesses must be contained by a professional."*

—GEORGE PLIMPTON

"Golf is a compromise between what your ego wants you to do, what experience tells you to do, and what your nerves let you do."

— BRUCE CRAMPTON

"An angry golfer is a loser. If he can't control himself, he can't control his shots."

—SAM SNEAD

"If a man can take five or six bogeys in a row, or a succession of flubbed shots without blowing his stack, he is capable of handling any situation."

—JIMMY DEMARET

"Enjoy the game. Happy golf is good golf."

—GARY PLAYER

The Nelson Scorecard

Major Championship Victories

Masters (1937, 1942)
U.S. Open (1939)
PGA Championship (1940, 1945)

Other Significant Achievements

Winner of 54 PGA events (in a short 13-year career)
11 consecutive victories in 1945
Vardon Trophy Winner (1939)

COURAGE

— Annika Sorenstam —

*I*n the late spring of 2003, Annika Sorenstam became the first female golfer to compete in a PGA tournament since the great Babe Zaharias had made an appearance some 58 years before. Her decision was not founded on making a statement for women's rights or inspired by feminist goals of equality, as much as it was on this: She wanted to test her game against the very best players the world could offer, and that meant teeing it up with the men. "This is a way to push myself to another level," she said. "This is for myself."

Sorenstam had dominated the women's tour the previous year, winning 11 titles, as well as her fifth Player of the Year Award and fifth Vare trophy (with a record-shattering 68.70 average). One of these titles was the Nabisco Championship, her fourth career major. In 2001, she had shot a 59 at the Standard Register Ping tournament, the first time that feat had ever been accomplished in professional women's golf. In fact, during that year she set or tied 30 LPGA records!

So Annika was looking for a new challenge—wanting to test her game against a new set of competitors by playing from the men's tees.

It took courage to make the decision to compete, knowing that many would resent her decision and knowing that a poor showing might reflect badly on her abilities and upon women's golf as a whole. But courage comes when you are willing to face all the obstacles in order to reach your goal. She worked out strenuously so she could increase her driving distance, improved her sometimes suspect putting, and learned to overcome her natural shyness so she could face the media onslaught that would come with her entry into a tournament that had never seen a woman as a competitor.

When all was said and done, Sorenstam did not win the tournament. But she did make a good showing, proving to herself that she could continue to improve and strengthen her game. It had taken great courage for her to venture into uncharted waters and test herself.

In life as in golf, it takes courage to do things we've never done before…or maybe never thought we could do. Often, when we step outside our comfort zone, we'll find strengths and abilities we didn't even know we had. And we'll never discover them unless we're willing to stretch our horizons.

"When you miss a shot, never think of what you did wrong. Come up to the next shot thinking of what you must do right."

—TOMMY ARMOUR

HOLE # 14

"The first thing I do after losing, regardless of whether I lost a close one because of a silly lapse or simply was snowed under by a rival running on a hot streak, is to forget it. I take a look at my calendar and start thinking about where we'll be playing next week, and I'll be playing next week, and I'll show 'em then!"

—NANCY LOPEZ

"A bad attitude is worse than a bad swing."

—PAYNE STEWART

"You must always be positive, because your body can only do what your brain sees."

—CHI CHI RODRIGUEZ

The Sorenstam Scorecard

Major Championship Victories
U.S. Women's Open (1995, 1996)
Nabisco Championship (2001, 2002)

Other Significant Achievements
Winner of 43 LPGA events
Rookie of the Year (1994)
Player of the Year (1995, 1997, 1998, 2001, 2002)
Vare Trophy (1995, 1996, 1998, 2001, 2002)

INTELLIGENCE

— Bobby Jones —

Someone once said that golf is "a thinking person's game." Truly, it is not a game that can be mastered through sheer strength, or quickness, or any other physical ability. Perhaps more than any other sport it demands the ability to think quickly and clearly. I suppose that is why many of the greatest golfers were also estimable thinkers. And none more so than Bobby Jones, the greatest amateur golfer who ever played the game.

Throughout his golfing career, Jones never played more than three months out of the year. Much of the rest of his time was dedicated to academic pursuits, and then later, to his law practice. Jones graduated from Georgia Tech in just three years, earning a degree in mechanical engineering. He followed that up with a degree in English literature from Harvard, and then he attended law school at Emory University, where he was able to withdraw after just his third semester and pass his bar exam. His ability to excel at both scientific and literary pursuits demonstrates that he was truly a renaissance man.

Along with immense natural skill, he brought that superior intellect to his golf game. Even though he only played golf part-time, he won 13 of the 21 major championships he entered during a seven-year stretch from 1923 to 1930. Then he retired at the top of his game.

Jones also used his mental prowess and creativity to help other golfers improve. His book *Bobby Jones on Golf* is still in print and provides helpful advice, masterfully explained. He also produced a series of instructional films that were widely used and acclaimed for their innovative teaching techniques.

The great ones have the ability to think their way around a golf course. Golf presents an ever-changing series of obstacles to overcome and decisions to be made. A poor decision can cost several strokes. The smart golfer must weigh his or her decisions carefully. Should I "go for it"—or would it be a better decision to lay up? How will the strength and direction of the wind affect this shot? Should I hit a 9-iron hard or an 8-iron softly? Should I putt the ball from the fringe or chip it? Every round demands numerous such decisions. And while we may not possess the awesome intelligence of a Bobby Jones, good golf demands that we use our head and play it smart.

In life as in golf, good decision-making is the key to a life of happiness and purpose. We'll improve our lives if we learn to take the time to think through the consequences of our actions and weigh carefully the best approach to resolving the struggles we face.

"A strong mind is one of the key components that separates the great from the good."

—GARY PLAYER

"Golf is a game of inches. The most important are those between the ears."

—ARNOLD PALMER

"Good players have the ability to think while they are competing. Most golfers are not thinking even when they believe they are. They are only worrying."

—HARVEY PENICK

The Jones Scorecard

Major Championship Victories

U.S. Open (1923, 1926, 1929, 1930)
British Open (1930)
U.S. Amateur (1924, 1925, 1927, 1928, 1930)
British Amateur (1930)

Other Significant Achievements

Only golfer ever to win four major championships in one calendar year

A Sense of Humor

— Lee Trevino —

Lee Trevino had a lot to laugh about. After all, it would have been hard to create a set of life experiences less likely to produce a championship-caliber golfer.

Trevino was born into poverty in a three-room shack in east Dallas. The house didn't even have plumbing. Raised by his mother and maternal grandfather, he never knew his father. By the age of five he was already at work supplementing the family income by laboring in the nearby cotton fields. He quit school in the eighth grade so he could make more money. The job he landed was at a driving range, where, between duties, he would hit hundreds of balls every day.

His talent began to blossom. Slowly but steadily, Trevino worked his way up out of poverty by caddying, playing for money, and taking on every challenger. Legend has it that sometimes he would even play the entire round using a pop bottle covered in gauze for a club if his opponent needed better odds. After a stint in the military, he played golf for money around Dallas and El Paso. "You don't know what pressure is," he said, "until you play for five bucks with only two in your pocket."

When he won the U.S. Open at Oak Hill in 1968 with a record-tying score, he was a complete unknown—but not for long. Trevino charmed galleries with his amazing shot-making ability, his rags-to-riches persona, and his rapid-fire wit.

Trevino was always making the gallery laugh. During competitive rounds he would make humorous comments, tell jokes, and sometimes even pull pranks on his fellow golfers. Once he threw a rubber snake at Jack Nicklaus during competition!

Surely one of the secrets to his success was that he was having fun. He realized how lucky he was to have risen out of poverty to the top of the world of professional golf, and the "Merry Mex" shared his joy by making us laugh.

In life as in golf, success starts with not taking ourselves too seriously. If we can laugh at ourselves and join in with the laughter of others, it will bring much more joy to our lives. Laughter helps us relax—and it gives us a better perspective on our lives.

"Keep your sense of humor. There's too much stress in the rest of your life to let bad shots ruin a game you're supposed to enjoy."

—Amy Alcott

"They call it golf because all the other four-letter words were taken."

—RAYMOND FLOYD

"My career started slowly, then tapered off."

—GARY MCCORD

The Trevino Scorecard

Major Championship Victories
U.S. Open (1968, 1971)
British Open (1971, 1972)
PGA Championship (1974, 1984)

Other Significant Achievements
Winner of 27 PGA Tour events
Vardon Trophy Winner (1970, 1974, 1980)

"There is no better game when you are in good company, and no worse game when you are in bad company."

—TOMMY BOLT

CREATIVITY

— Gene Sarazen —

At first glance, Gene Sarazen was unlikely to be one of the greatest golfers of all time. He was a mere five-foot-five and had a swing that was anything but graceful. But he was a fierce competitor who used the gifts he had to the fullest.

Sarazen is best known for three things:

First, for what is probably the most famous shot in the history of golf. In the 1935 Masters he trailed Craig Wood by three strokes with only four holes to go. Arriving at the par-five fifteenth hole, he hit a solid drive into the middle of the fairway. Then, pulling out his four wood for his second shot, Sarazen took dead aim at the flag. He struck the ball perfectly, and it carried over the pond in front of the green, took a couple of hops, and rolled into the hole for a rare double-eagle. He went on to win the tournament.

Second, for being one of only a handful of players to complete the career Grand Slam—a victory in each of the major championships.

Finally, for his creativity. He constantly used his intelligence and imagination to find ways to improve his game. In 1929, taking a tip from baseball great Ty Cobb, Sarazen developed what was probably the first weighted practice club, which helped him improve his swing and his distance. Then, a couple years later, Howard Hughes was teaching him how to fly a plane. Sarazen noticed the way the tail adjusted downward during takeoff. After pondering this, he realized that these aerodynamics could help create a club that would perform better out of sand traps. He perfected it by adding a bunch of solder to the flange of his pitching wedge. With that, the modern sand wedge was born!

In life as in golf, creativity and imagination are important for overcoming obstacles. When we find ourselves in a difficult place, it often helps if we can think outside the box. We'll find new ways to overcome obstacles and new ideas that will bring fresh perspective.

"What other people may find in poetry or art museums, I find in the flight of a good drive."

—ARNOLD PALMER

HOLE #17

"As I get older, I try to think of the bad things that happen to me on the golf course as 'tests.' They're not hurdles; they're not bad marks or punishments. They're the things I need in my life, things that bring me back to reality."

—FRANK BEARD

"When I get out on that green carpet called a fairway and manage to poke the ball right down the middle, my surroundings look like a touch of heaven on earth."

—JIMMY DEMARET

The Sarazen Scorecard

Major Championship Victories
U.S. Open (1922, 1932)
PGA Championship (1922, 1923, 1933)
British Open (1932)
Masters (1935)

Other Significant Achievements
Winner of 38 events on the PGA Tour

PERSEVERANCE

— Bernhard Langer —

Steve Ballesteros once said that the secret of successful golf is to forget. Perhaps no one in golf has shown the ability to "let the past remain in the past" and move on better than Bernhard Langer, the greatest German golfer of all time.

Langer's résumé contains a lot of highlights. But between those highlights have been some dark moments that might have done other golfers in. Throughout his career, Langer struggled with the "yips"—a malady that produces a jerky movement preventing the golfer from achieving a smooth putting stroke. For many, the onset of the yips means the end of a golfing career, but Langer has always come back, finding different—sometimes unorthodox—ways to overcome his struggles. Four separate times he overcame serious putting woes that could have meant the end of his competitive career, demonstrating over and over the perseverance needed to make the necessary adjustments and keep working on his game. He simply didn't give up.

In the final round of the 1991 Ryder Cup, Langer battled back from the brink of defeat by winning three of the final five holes to tie his opponent going into the last hole. There, Langer faced a six-foot putt. If he holed it, it would mean that Europe would retain the Cup for another two years. If not, it would go to the U.S. Talk about pressure! When his putt narrowly missed, handing victory—and the Cup— to the Americans, you could see the agony in his face and posture. He was devastated.

Many commentators wondered how long the missed putt would haunt Langer and whether his game would ever recover. But only seven days later, he was victorious in the German Masters, proof of his mental strength, his courage, his perseverance, and his faith. Langer, a devout Christian, pointed to the strength his faith gave him, strength that helped him through defeat and disappointment. In 1993 Langer won the Masters tournament in the United States, the final round of which was played that year on Easter Sunday. "Winning on Easter Sunday," he said, "added a very special meaning to me personally."

In life as in golf, we will often find ourselves tempted to give up when we feel overwhelmed by life's challenges and setbacks. But those who find the strength to persevere will find peace and fulfillment again on the other side of even their most daunting obstacles and difficulties. As Winston Churchill once intoned, "Never, never, never, give up!"

"I expect to make at least seven mistakes a round. Therefore, when I make a bad shot, I don't worry about it. It's just one of those seven."

—WALTER HAGEN

"The phrase 'where there's a will there's a way' comes to mind when I think of Bernhard. He was always fidgeting with weights and lofts in search of better results. He took it upon himself to find a way to putt and his enormous success over the years shows that his hard work has paid off."

—BEN CRENSHAW

"The toughest thing for most people to learn in golf is to accept bad holes— and then forget about them."

—GARY PLAYER

The Langer Scorecard

Major Championship Victories
Masters (1985, 1993)

Other Significant Achievements
Winner of 3 PGA Tour events
Winner of 42 European PGA Tour events
Order of Merit Leader (1981, 1984)
European Vardon Trophy (1981, 1984)
European Tour Golfer of the Year (1985, 1993)

GOLF AND THE SPIRITUAL JOURNEY

I do quite a bit of praying on the golf course. Much of it is along the lines of "Please don't let that five-iron shot land in the water." My other prayers are a bit more spiritual in nature.

There is something about being out on the golf course that seems to put me in mind of the greater realities. Over the years, theologians and preachers and writers have offered a lot of metaphors that reflect various aspects of the spiritual journey. Consider, for example, *Pilgrim's Progress,* in which traveling or pilgrimage is used to picture spiritual realities. Well, what if Christian, the main character in that classic book, had been a golfer? Couldn't he have learned some important lessons from a round at his local course? By paying attention to some of the aspects of this game, we just might find that they mirror some of the joys and struggles of becoming a spiritually mature person.

CHARACTER

Golf is a game of character. If you want to learn a lot about somebody, just play a round of golf with them. You'll learn quite a bit about the extent of their patience, their ability to deal with disappointment, their gracefulness in triumph and defeat, and especially their honesty. This sometimes maddening game is a test for all these facets of the human character and many more...and a microcosm of the way the world around us tests us. If we can't say no to cheating by reporting a lower score than we actually managed, if we can't resist the temptation to "improve our lie," then we may find ourselves falling short in some of life's greater and more defining tests.

Theologians talk a lot about law and grace. Golf is a delicate balance between these two realities. It is law, in that it is based upon a set of rules you must accept if you are to play the game as it is intended to be played. Of course you can cheat. You can make sure no one is watching, then gently nudge the ball into a better lie. You can explain away the whiff as "a practice swing." You can allow yourself a seventh mulligan. Sometimes, as in life, God is the only witness to your petty little crime. But in the end, you are really cheating only yourself.

The rules are created to make the game more fair, more enjoyable, more challenging. The rule book of golf can seem overwhelming to master, filled as it is with regulations both general and trivial, some of which do seem awfully persnickety. But it exists to give the game structure and limits, to help you judge your actual improvement, and to make the experience of playing with others easier. The rules of golf give the game its meaning. And what can compare with the feeling of "taking your medicine" and still managing to get a good score? Doesn't it feel much more fulfilling to use a five-wood to escape from an all-but-impossible lie than to just kick the ball over to where you have an easier shot?

*"Golf puts a man's character on the anvil and his richest qualities—
patience, poise, and restraint—to the flame."*

—Billy Casper

*"There are only two things in the world you've got to do
with your head down—golf and praying."*

ENJOYING A FRESH START

But golf isn't all about the rules. Golf reflects grace, in that every hole is a new challenge. With each new hole, no matter how badly you did on the last one, you get a fresh start—a new beginning. In fact, each shot offers opportunity for redemption. If you've duck-hooked a two-iron into the woods, it still remains possible that your next shot may put you right back where you need to be. If you leave your approach shot short, it's still possible to score a birdie if your chip has the right distance and direction.

Golf is a game where you learn you should never give up. Just when you're most discouraged, you may surprise yourself. We all hit shots now and then that can only be described as miraculous. In fact, I think this is one of the things that keeps me coming back to this sometimes frustrating game—the reality that once in a while I'll hit a shot almost as good as one that Tiger Woods might hit. (Just once in a while, mind you.) During any round, I'll probably hit a shot or two (or make a putt) rivaling what even the most talented professional might hit.

Isn't life the same way? We screw up, we make mistakes large and small, and we don't follow through—but despite all that, we can get a new start if we choose. We don't have to be hamstrung by the past. Whatever we might have done, we can be forgiven and get a fresh start. A large part of spiritual maturity is realizing that this newness must be grasped again and again. We will continually play the game of life inadequately, but we shouldn't get so distracted by

our mistakes that we can't enjoy what is before us and strive for a higher goal for ourselves.

DISCIPLINE

This brings me to another parallel between the spiritual life and golf. In both these endeavors, we'll become more comfortable and more skilled only as we discipline ourselves toward improvement. You don't become a championship golfer overnight—it requires years of focus, practice, learning, and attention. It's the same way with spiritual maturity. It comes as we make it a priority in our lives. We have to care enough to put in the time to improve.

Remember how strange the golf grip felt when you first learned the game? Now it probably feels natural. It's the same with cultivating the traits that make us a better person. Act as you know you should, instead of just doing what comes naturally. Trust the wisdom of those who have experienced more than you and accept what they have to offer. We can often learn a great deal from those who have walked the course ahead of us…and spiritual mentors are as necessary as swing coaches in golf.

ACCEPTING THE UNEXPECTED

But no matter how good our intentions, things don't always work out the way we think they should. Life isn't fair. Shanks happen.

Golf, like life, is full of the unexpected. You never know what might be just around the corner. Sometimes a golfing calamity is birthed

from our own foolishness (too much club, too little club, mis-hits, trying to power the ball to get a few extra yards). Other times our calamity comes about through no fault of our own (an unreadable break, a bad bounce, a poorly kept course). Either way, we must play the ball where it lies.

A badly hit shot may turn out okay. Not long ago I hit a horrible slice off the sixteenth tee at a local course. The ball swooped right in a slow arch like a drunken sparrow—until it hit a tree dead-on and ricocheted right back into the center of the fairway. After the shot I'd hit, I didn't deserve that result. But I was grateful for how it helped my score on that hole.

Of course, it works the other way as well—a beautifully struck shot climbs slowly like a jet at takeoff, lands beautifully just in front of the green, bounces once—and then, on the second bounce, jumps erratically to the right and into a deep bunker, where it comes to rest right under the lip. Wait a minute! How did that happen? Well, you can curse your bad luck all the rest of the round, but wouldn't it be better to focus your energy on figuring out how to play that bunker shot?

You just gotta play it as it lies.

JOY AND THANKFULNESS

Of course, the biggest reason I play golf is for the sheer joy of it. I love the sound of the birds and the wind in the trees, the stately *clonk* of a well-hit driver, and the rattle of the ball as it finds the bottom of the cup. I love the challenge of trying to figure out how to play the next shot—and occasionally making exactly the right decision. I love the camaraderie of playing with friends and rooting for each other, even when we are opponents, or the simple pleasure of playing alone on a slow autumn afternoon when I can play two balls and compete against myself. (This is also the only time I can count on winning!) I love the wondrous beauty of a well-groomed course, a perfect balance of man-made artistic imagination and the native beauty of God's good world. When I can relax and not be too focused on how well I am scoring, I find a simple peace in my heart as I chase my ball through 18 holes.

And I am grateful. I am thankful I can play this marvelous and sometimes exasperating game surrounded by the beauty of God's creation. I find myself glad to be alive. And isn't this also the ultimate secret to the spiritual life? To be thankful for what you have been given and to love the One who has given it to you?

So pay attention to the game of golf. You just might learn something that will help you become the kind of person you really want to be.